Celebrating You:
Graduate!

THIS IS YOUR DAY

NAME _____

SCHOOL _____

CITY _____

DATE _____

celebrating you:

The
Graduate

What a Great Year!

Memories

Memories I will treasure . . .

Friends

Friends I will always remember:

Teachers

Teachers who rocked my world:

The Big Day!

How I Celebrated

Who was there
to celebrate with me...

the *Future*

where will I go
from here...

what are my goals & objectives...

Secrets of Success

May God grant you
according to your
heart's desire,
and fulfill all
your purpose.
We will rejoice in
your salvation,
and in the name
of our God
we will set up
our banners!
May the Lord fulfill
all your petitions.

Psalm 20:4-5 NKJV

twisting of

ungraceful
v. -er n.
a fine mist
nd forth in

en fully; to
force apart;

gence in an

ous, lively.
ter in small
nall drops.
ace.
A tooth-like
heel.
m tree with
d soft wood.
nergetic

device

for spit.

spitz (spits) n. A small dog with
curls over its back.
splash (splash) v. To spatter a
or soil with liquid; to make a spl
n. **splashy** adj.
splash-down (splash´doun´) n
of a missile or spacecraft in th
spleen (splēn) n., Anat. A hi
flattened organ which filters and
loc below the diaphragm.

splen

nifi

splic

ove

splin

or

sp

splot

sh

splu

spitting sound. **splutter** n.
soil

device

> **Genius is seldom**
> **recognized**
> **for what it is:**
> **a great capacity**
> **for hard work.**
>
> *Henry Ford*

Success

Secrets of Success

Reputation is what
people think you are.
Character is
who you really are.
Take care of your character
and your reputation
will take care of itself.

Author Unknown

The secret of joy in work
is contained in one word
— excellence.
To know how to
do something well
is to enjoy it.

Pearl S. Buck

Secrets of Success

To achieve the impossible, you must think the absurd; look where everyone else has looked, but see what no one else has seen.

Author Unknown

Success

The remarkable truth is
that our choices matter,
not just to us and
our own destiny but,
amazingly, to God Himself
and the universe He rules.

Philip Yancey

Secrets
of
Success

Along the way you will stumble, and perhaps even fall;
but that, too, is normal and to be expected.
Get up, get back on your feet, chastened but wiser,
and continue on down the road.

~ Arthur Ashe

Cherish your visions
and your dreams,
as they are the children
of your soul;
the blueprints of your
ultimate achievements.

Napoleon Hill

Secrets of my Success

Take your everyday,
ordinary life—
your sleeping, eating,
going-to-work,
and walking-around life—
and place it before God
as an offering.
Embracing what God does
for you is the best thing
you can do for him.

Romans 12:1 MSG

Success

Additional copies of this book and
other titles from ELM HILL BOOKS
are available from your local bookstore.

Other titles in the Celebrating You series:
Celebrating You: I Love You, Mom
Celebrating You: I Love You, Dad

For additions, deletions, corrections,
or clarifications in future editions of this text,
please contact Paul Shepherd,
Editor in Chief for ELM HILL BOOKS.
Email pshepherd@elmhillbooks.com.

Products from ELM HILL BOOKS may be purchased in bulk
for educational, business, fundraising, or sales promotional use.
For information, please email
SpecialMarkets@ThomasNelson.com